A Journey From Ashes To Poetry

Entangled thoughts woven into words

Manju Srivastava

BookLeaf Publishing

India | USA | UK

Made with ❤ on the BookLeaf Publishing Platform
www.bookleafpub.in
www.bookleafpub.com

Dedication

This book is dedicated to everyone who knows what mental disturbance is. Though some of us have started talking about this helplessness lately. However, it still is a taboo in our society. I, myself have seen people not ready to accept that they need therapy.

And ironically, many of us even don't know that they are suffering from mental illness.

So, I've created poems on various facets of mental illness and healing journey.

I'm sure it will be relatable to many and this book is for all of them.

Also, I am dedicating this book to my family and friends.

Thank you everyone for encouraging me to write!

Preface

Have you seen anyone around who is sleepy but struggling to sleep, guilty but not able to keep up with their daily routine, always apologetic, avoid meeting people, finding discomfort in crowded place??? Maybe they need help. However, neither you nor they are aware of their situation... And thereby there is a dire need of awareness on mental illness in our society.

Let's build an inclusive environment for everyone so that each individual can live freely and happily, irrespective of their abilities.

Acknowledgements

I was thinking to take this challenge and write my book but procrastinating. And then one day got a message - "I want your book to be published this year" along with bookleaf's instagram ad.
And that day I finally enrolled for bookleaf's writing challenge...
Thank you Yuga ma'am for pushing me one step ahead towards my goal.
My son kept reminding me that "Mumma, you are running late for the challenge, write and submit it as soon as possible."
Thank you Shaarav for always being there.
Though these two names deserve special mention, there are many others who have always motivated me some or other way.
Thanks to all my near and dear ones...

1. The Weight of Anxiety

It sits like a stone upon your chest,
a restless whisper, never at rest.
A racing pulse, a fleeting breath,
a silent fear that speak of death.

It weaves a web inside your mind,
a maze of doubts, cruelly designed.
Each step you take, the echoes grow,
a voice that tells you, "*No, no, no.*"

You count the steps, you pace the floor,
a mind that knocks on every door.
What if you fall? What if they see?
what if you're not who you should be?

Your thoughts run wild, they twist, they turn,
they flicker fast, they scorch, they burn.
You try to rest, but sleep doesn't stay,
the weight of what-ifs fills your day.

You chase the calm, beg for peace,
but still, the worries never cease.
Yet in the storm, you plant your feet,
a flicker of hope, a steady beat.

One breath, one step - you take your time,
unraveling fears that once troubled you in line.
Though the weight still remain strong,
but you are learning - you belong!

2. Racing Thoughts

The clock strikes one but your mind is awake,
a restless tide which is difficult to break.
A whisper turns into a roar,
a single thought becomes a war.

Did I say too much today?
or not enough - did I betray?
You wear a mask of smile that's so thin,
isn't the chaos screaming deep within?

A future built on "what-ifs" high,
a past replayed like blackened sky.
Your mind rewinds the whole twists and turns,
each fleeting thought, it scars, it burns.

You try to breathe, you count to ten,
but here they come, those doubts again.
A tangled web, a storm untamed,
each fear you've named, then named again.

The clock strikes four and your body is still,
thoughts climb, they rise and they fill.
But dawn will break and light will show,
that not all racing thoughts must grow.

3. Silent Battles

A fake yet perfect smile, on which the world believes,
but the wounds within, no one sees.
A laughter rings, light and free,
however, deep inside, there is an ongoing fight unseen.

An unwanted weight that tucked away,
a storm keeps raging night and day.
myriad scars to show and uncountable wounds to trace,
but there's a quite war, which is inevitable to erase.

Kindness and love for all,
yet drown alone behind your walls.
You might seem strong and bright,
but it is heartbreaking to know how you break at night.

For silent battles, fierce yet true,
are fought by hearts that still push through.

4. The War Inside

There is a continuous war inside of you,
an ongoing skirmish seen by only a few.
No swords, no shields, no battle cries,
yet every day, a part of you dies.

The frontline is in your mind,
a place where peace is hard to find.
Doubts like daggers pierce your chest,
anxiety marches, never rests.

Depression lingers, dark and deep,
a shadow pulling you to sleep.
You try to fight, you try to find balance to stand,
but fear grips you tightly by the hand.

There are wounds that may cut quite deep,
but you neither bow nor weep.
For even warrior battle scars,
and even darkness yields to stars.

5. Learning to Breathe Again

You've held your breath for far too long,
carrying burdens, silent and strong.
The weight of the past, the fear of the now,
have stolen your voice, yet you don't know how.

Your heart beats fast, your hands grow tight,
lost in the echoes of endless night.
You shrink, you hide, afraid to be seen,
trapped in a world where you've never been free.

But listen--softly, the wind still sings,
the sun still rises, the sparrow still wings.
The air is waiting, the sky is wide,
hope is a whisper right by your side.

So part your lips, inhale the light,
let go of the battles you've fought in the night.
One breath, then two-slow and true,
the world is here, still waiting for you.

6. The Art of Letting Go

Letting go is not a fall,
neither a failure nor a call.
To erase the past, to break, to bend,
but rather, learning how to mend.

It starts in whispers, soft yet true,
a voice inside reminding you
that holding on to what has been
won't change the now or where you've been.

You trace the memories, bright and wild,
some full of sorrow, some soft and mild.
They shaped your heart, they wrote your name,
but clinging tight won't keep them the same.

So loosen your grip, release the weight,
not every loss is laced with fate.
Some things must leave, some doors must close,
for you to bloom, for you to grow.

The wind still blows, the rivers flow,
and so must you, just take it slow.
For peace is not in holding tight,
but in trusting life to make things right.

7. Scars That Tell Stories

Every scar upon your skin,
every mark you hide within,
is not a wound, not just a pain,
but proof that you have lived through heavy rain.

They narrate tales of battles fought,
of lessons learned, of strength well-wrought.
Each line, each bruise, each faded ache,
a chapter that you did not break.

The world may stare, may never see,
the weight you've borne so silently.
But scars are maps, not chains the bind,
they show how far you've come, no need to look behind.

So wear them proudly, don't turn away,
they shaped the soul you are today.
Even broken things can shine,
and every scar, a start divine.

8. Small Victories

You woke up today -- that is enough,
though the night behind was long and rough.
You took a breath, you faced the light,
a quiet win, a spark of fight.

You got out of bed, your feet met the floor,
a step so small, yet worth so much more.
You spoke when silence felt so safe,
you tried again -- you found your faith.

No trumpets sound, no banners wave,
yet here you stand, so strong, so brave.
Because healing comes in steps, not flight,
and small victories still shine bright.

9. Sunrise After the Storm

The night was long, the winds ran wild,
the thunder roared, the sky untiled.
You braved the rough weather, you felt it sting,
but storms don't last, they take it all back whatever they
bring.

Once the world was dark, the path was unclear,
each step was weighed with doubt and fear.
But even as the tempest grew,
something inside still carried you.

And now, behold -- the sky turns gold,
the dawn ignites the stories told.
Each drop that fell, each tear, each ache,
has paved the road that you now take.

The storm has passed, yet you remain,
not lost, not weak, reborn from pain.
For even in the fiercest night,
the sun still rises, bathed in light.

10. You Are Not Alone

I see the weight you try to hide,
some quiet yet heavy storms you burried inside.
The faster-paced world cannot see,
but don't worry -- you're safe with me.

You wear a beautiful smile, but I can tell,
the wars you fought, the drak nights you fell.
Your fears are evident, but you have to go with the flow,
the pain you carry -- just let it go.

Who said that you're too much,
you're not beyond a helping touch.
Here's a space for you, a hand to hold,
ear that listens, every story untold.

So when the nights feel cold and long,
when echoes tell you don't belong.
Remember this -- you're not alone,
you are seen, you are known.

11. The Light Within Me

The path was too steep,
and I lost myself in shadows deep.
Everything around grew cold and unkind,
yet there was a spark that refused to die.

I broke badly, I fell apart,
but somewhere deep within my heart,
a voice rose, feeble but so true --
saying, *You'll make it through.*

Despite the scars and ache,
and every fear that tried to break,
my inner glow refused to fade,
a fire in the dark it made.

The thunderstorm could not steal what ignites inside,
and no wave could drown the will to rise.
Because even when the night is long,
the light within me still shines strong.

12. A Love Letter to Myself

Dear Me,

I see your heart, the weight you bear,
the quiet battles, the silent prayers.
The days you've stumbled, lost, unsure,
yet still, you rise and endure.

I know the fears you hide so deep,
the nights you toss, the tears you keep.
But through it all, you've learned to grow,
a gentle strength the world won't know.

So here's my vow, my self embrace,
to give you love, to help you act on your pace.
To speak to you in kinder ways,
to be the warmth on colder days.

You don't have to chase, don't have to prove,
just be yourself, that is enough.
Breathe, rest, and let life flow,
you are loved, you should know.

With love, always,
Me.

13. The Common Stigma

They call it a phase, a fleeting tide,
a battle fought but brushed aside.
"*Just cheer up*", they often say,
as if the storm will drift away.

They see the smile, the mask in place,
yet miss the cracks we dare not trace.
The weight we carry, the silent screams,
reduced to whispers, lost in themes.

They label us *fragile, too weak to cope*,
yet fail to see the strength in hope.
For every tear that falls unseen,
a warrior stands where pain has been.

Mental scars are real as bone,
yet still, we fight this war alone.
Not broken souls, not minds astray,
just hearts that heal in their own way.

So listen close, look past the guise,
see the truth behind the eyes.
No shame, no fear - just voices strong,
breaking the stigma we've worn too long.

14. Listen Before You Judge

You see the smile, the laugh, the fake face,
but not the battles they erase.
You hear their words, yet miss the plea,
a heart that aches so silently.

You see the anger, the distant gaze,
but not the nights lost in a haze.
The load, the pressure is not at all thin,
yet still, they hide it deep within.

It's easy to point, to place the blame,
to speak undertone, to cast a name.
But wounds aren't healed by careless eyes,
or hearts that fail to realize.

So pause for a moment, breathe, be still,
hold your judgement, change your will.
For every soul you fail to see,
could be a soul who just needs *peace*.

15. A World That Understands

Imagine a world gentle and kind,
where no one fears to speak their mind.
Where hearts are met with grace,
and no one hides or feels out of place.

A world where pain is not disguised,
where teary eyes aren't criticized.
Where asking for help is believed as strong,
and every soul knows they belong.

Where minds are tended, just like the skin,
and healing starts from deep within.
Where care is given, without playing blame game,
and no one wears a whispered name.

Someday, I hope this world will be,
a place of light for you and me.
Where love will be louder than demands -
a world that listens, understands.

16. Behind Closed Doors

Behind closed doors, where no one sees,
a silent war brings weary knees.
A smile fades, a mask comes down,
a heart sinks deep, afraid of drown.

Everybody sees the strength and perhaps grace,
but never tears that stain this place.
The battles fought in lonely nights,
the untold fears, the quiet fights.

A heavy weight, a hidden ache,
a robust soul that tries, but sometimes breaks.
Yet out in crowd, they stand tall,
as if they do not fight at all.

So look beyond what meets the eye,
not every pain is seen to cry.
Be kind and lend your hand -
for struggles live where few will stand.

17. Breaking the Silence

The thoughts you carry, deep and strong,
have lived in shadows for too long.
An unseen pain, a silent plea,
a story trapped, longing to be free.

Some tell you, "*Hide it, don't complain,*"
as if your heart should bear the strain.
As if the mind should heal alone,
without a voice, without a home.

But pain unspoken only grows,
a silent storm that no one knows.
And healing starts, so small, so true,
the moment words break through to you.

So share your thoughts, let echoes rise,
now remove the mask, no need for lies.
For every voice that dares to share,
can build a world that learns to care.

18. Healing Is Not Linear

No, healing is not just a climb,
it's neither a steady path nor a race with time.
Past keep calling you back,
and the heart keep aching for what it lack.

Yes, healing has its twists, turns and sways,
some nights feel lost, some bright like days.
You take a step, you rise so high,
then fall again and wonder why.

Some wounds ache, then fade, then burn,
some lessons take their time to learn.
Some days you dance, feel light, feel free,
some days the past doesn't let you be.

But this does not mean you have failed,
your ship is robust, though winds assail.
Despite several falls and scars,
you're still stronger than many others are.

This path is tough, rough and unclear,
keep walkin on - release the fear.
For healing isn't just a climb,
it's finding peace, in your own time.

19. When The Mind Says 'Rest'

The world keeps moving, fast and loud,
pushing you somewhere, and you lost in the crowd.
You might feel - you shouldn't slow your stride,
but what if you need a breath inside?

Your mind grows heavy, thoughts run deep,
you might need some space or quality sleep.
Yet guilt creeps in, a quiet fear -
"If I stop now, will I disappear?"

But rest is not a sign of loss,
it has its ample pros and no cons.
It's where the weary soul rewinds,
don't forget, strength is found in calm minds.

So close your eyes, release the weight,
the world can pause - the rest can wait.
Because healing starts when you allow
yourself to breathe, to rest, for now.

20. Creating a Life That Feels Right

They tell you how to live, to be,
a list of rules, a lock, no key.
A path well-trodden, safe and tight,
but does it make your spirit light?

You weren't born to fit a mold,
to chase a dream that feels so cold.
Your heart beats wild, it sings its own,
a rhythm meant stand alone.

So build a life that feels like you,
where passion shines in all you do.
Set boundaries firm, yet soft with grace,
let only love fill up your space.

Surround yourself with souls that see
the beauty in your way to be.
For joy is found where truth takes flight,
a life lived full, a life lived right.

21. Giving Back and Spreading Light

I once was lost in shadows deep,
a weary soul, too tired to weep.
I walked through storms, I broke, I bled,
yet somehow, still, I rose instead.

The road was long, the nights unkind,
but healing taught me what to find -
Not just the strength to stand once more,
but hands to lift, to help, restore.

For now, I see in others' eyes
the same old ache, the same goodbyes.
And if my voice, my scars, my past
can show them that pain won't always last.

Then let me speak, let kindness grow,
let love be louder than the woe.
For what we give is what remains -
a spark of light through someone's pain.

No path is walked, no wound is healed,
without a hand, a heart revealed.

So here I stand, no longer small,
to spread the light that saved me all.